Use the secret code to solve the riddle.

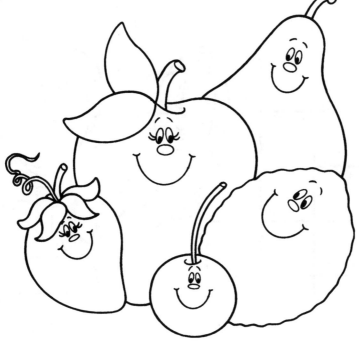

What kind of fruit do we find in history?

⬡ ◯ △ ▽ ⅄

Secret Code

⅄ = S   ◯ = A   ▽ = E

⬡ = D   △ = T

13

Use the word list to solve the crossword puzzle.

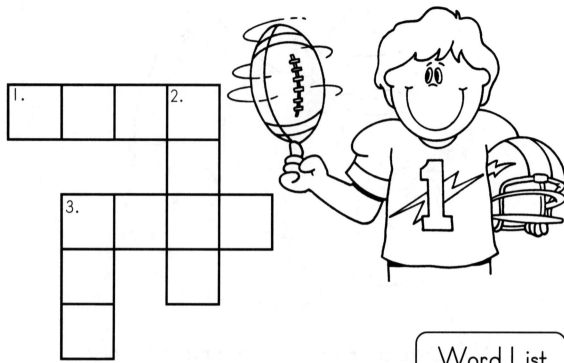

Across

1. Football is a fun game to _____.
3. Football players throw and kick a
   ____.

Word List

play

big

ball

yell

Down

2. The fans ____ and cheer.
3. Most football players are _____
   and strong.

Use the secret code to solve the riddle.

What animal never leaves its home but travels everywhere?

A ___ ___ ___ ___ ___

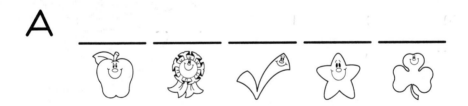

Use the word list to solve the crossword puzzle.

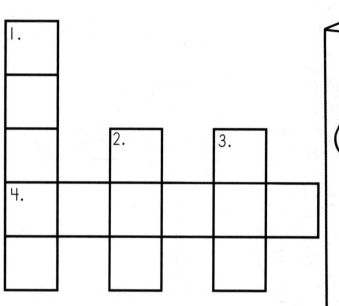

Across

4. Sam had a bowl of _____ for breakfast.

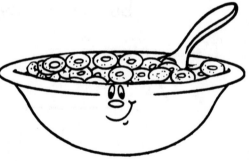

Down

1. A drink made from fruit is called _____.

2. You _____ bacon in a pan.

3. The eggs are cooking in the _____.

Word List
cereal
fry
juice
pan

Use the secret code to answer the riddle.

What pool is not good for swimming?

A _____ _____ _____   _____ _____ _____ _____

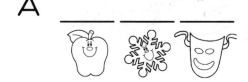 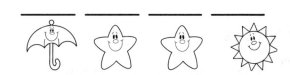

Secret Code

= L   = O   = A

= C   = R   = P

Use the word list to solve the crossword puzzle.

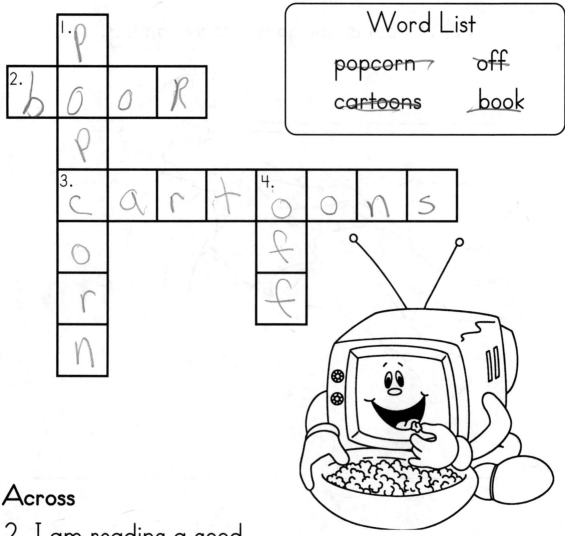

Word List

popcorn   off

cartoons   book

1. p
2. b o o R
   p
3. c a r t o o n s
   o   f
   r   f
   n

Across

2. I am reading a good _____.

3. I watch ____ on Saturday mornings.

Down

1. We eat white and fluffy ____.

4. Turn the TV ____ when you leave.

Use the secret code to solve the riddle.

What kind of cup is good to eat?

A <u>C</u> <u>u</u> <u>p</u> <u>C</u> <u>A</u> <u>K</u> <u>E</u>

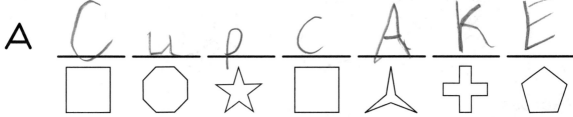

Secret Code

⬡ = U	⬠ = E	⑃ = A			
☐ = C	✚ = K	☆ = P			

Use the word list to solve the crossword puzzle.

Word List

wash   soap

pans   towel

Across

1. Dry the dishes with a

   ____.

3. Rinse the ____ off

   the dishes.

Down

2. It's your turn to ____

   the dishes.

4. Sometimes you have to

   scrub the pots and

   ____.

Use the secret code to solve the riddle.

What card game do cats like to play?

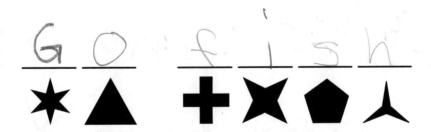

G O   f i s h
★ ▲   ✚ ✖ ⬟ ⅄

Secret Code

⬟ = S	▲ = O	✖ = I
✚ = F	★ = G	⅄ = H

Use the word list to solve the crossword puzzle.

Word List

| cut | tools | ax | nail |

Across

3. An ____ is used to chop down a tree.

4. My father has many ____ in his tool box.

Down

1. You pound a ____ with a hammer.

2. My dad uses a saw to ____ wood.

Use the secret code to solve the riddle.

What kind of nut has nothing inside?

Ha, Ha.

A D O U G H N U T

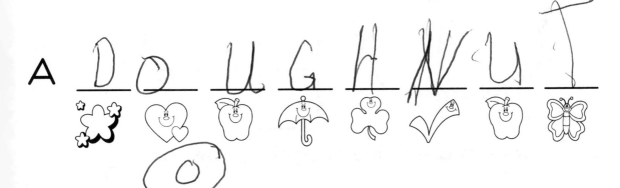

Secret Code

🍀 = H   🍎 = U   🦋 = T   ✓ = N

🌟 = D   ❤️ = O   ☂️ = G

23   © Carson-Dellosa Publ. CD-6875

Use the word list to solve the crossword puzzle.

Word List

eggs   bird   tree   twigs

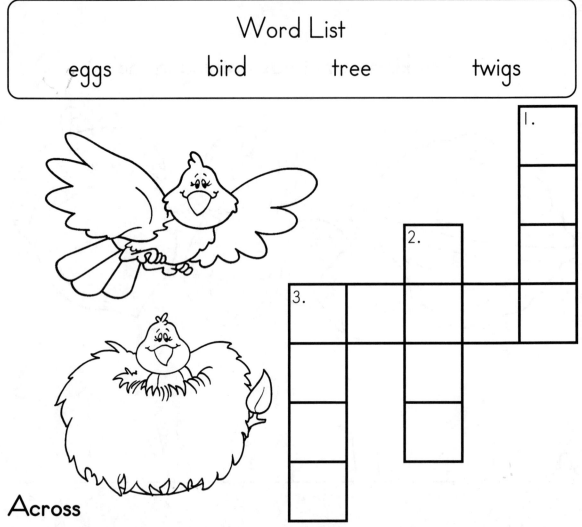

Across

3. Most nests are made of string, straw, and _____.

Down

1. Birds lay _____ in their nests.

2. An animal that flies and lays eggs is a _____.

3. The bird built its nest in a _____.

Use the secret code to solve the riddle.

What kind of cat never meows?

A <u>catfish</u>

✛ ⬡ △ ✦ ○ ⅄ ☐

Secret Code

✦ = F   ⬡ = A   ☐ = H   ○ = I

△ = T   ⅄ = S   ✛ = C

Use the word list to solve the crossword puzzle.

Word List

fur   bone   bark   leash

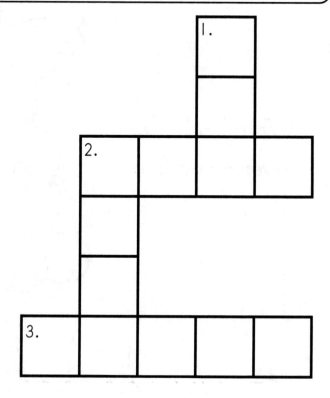

Across

2. Dogs like to ____.

3. A dog must wear a ____ before it can go for a walk.

Down

1. A dog is covered with ____.

2. A dog likes to chew on a ____.

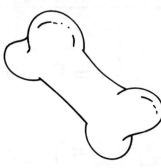

Use the secret code to solve the riddle.

Which side of a chicken
has the most feathers?

THE

O u T S I D e

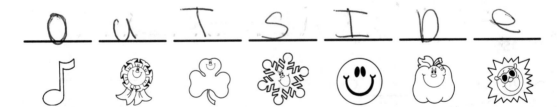

Secret Code

☺ = I	= U	= T	= E
= D	♪ = O	= S	

27

Use the word list to solve the crossword puzzle.

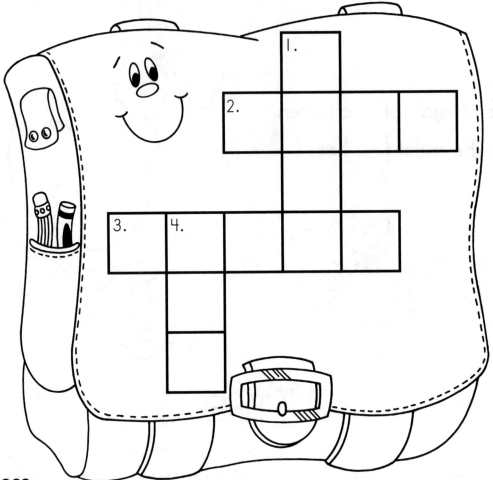

Across

2. Open your ____ and read.

3. You write on ____.

Down

1. You do your homework at ____.

4. Raise your hand to ____ a

   question.

Word List

home

book

ask

paper

28

Use the secret code to solve the riddle.

What's the best thing to put in a chocolate cake?

___ ___ ___ ___   ___ ___ ___ ___ ___

Secret Code

☂ = H   ✔ = U   🌼 = T   ❄ = R

⭐ = Y   ☁ = O   🏵 = E

Use the word list to solve the crossword puzzle.

Across

2. I like to put ____ on my toast.

Down

1. I like peanut butter and ____.

2. Freshly baked ____ smells wonderful!

3. A toaster turns bread into ____.

Word List

jelly

butter

toast

bread

Use the secret code to solve the riddle.

What would you get if you crossed
a cow and a tadpole?

A ___ ___ ___ ___ ___ ___ ___ ___

Secret Code

🍎 = L   🍀 = U   ⭐ = F   🌼 = R

☂ = B   ☁ = O   ❄ = G

Use the word list to solve the crossword puzzle.

Across

1. Rock-and-roll is my favorite type of ____.

3. You write music with ____.

5. My brother plays the drums in a ____.

Down

2. I like to ____ Christmas carols.

4. I heard my favorite ____ on the radio.

Word List

song

band

notes

music

sing

Use the secret code to solve the riddle.

What kind of coat won't keep you warm?

A _____ _____ _____ _____ OF _____ _____ _____ _____ _____

(△ ⬠ ■ ⬟) (∧ ■ ☆ ✚ ⬟)

Secret Code

■ = A	∧ = P	⬟ = T	✚ = N
△ = C	⬠ = O	☆ = I	

Use the word list to solve the crossword puzzle.

Word List

mice	meow	cat
tree	dog	

Across

2. The cat says ____.

4. A cat will sometimes climb a ____.

Down

1. A cat will run from a ____.

2. Cats like to chase ____.

3. A kitten grows up to be a ____.

34

Use the secret code to solve the riddle.

What kind of cake does not taste good?

A ___ ___ ___ _K_ ___   OF   ___ ___ ___ ___ _P_

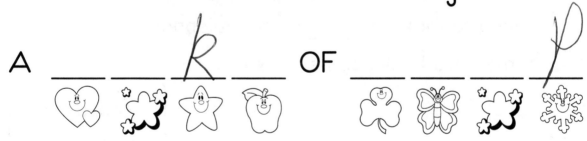

Secret Code

= E   = A   = K   = S

= C   = O   = P

Use the word list to solve the crossword puzzle.

Across

1. I need to make a _____ on the telephone.
3. Sometimes I talk, sometimes I _____.

Down

1. You need _____ to use the pay phone.
2. When the phone _____, I answer it.
4. I like to _____ on the phone.

Word List

rings
listen
talk
coins
call

Use the secret code to solve the riddle.

What do you call
a parrot?

A __ __ __ __ __

__ __ __ __ __

Secret Code

 = Y   = B  = W   = I

= D = O = R

Use the word list to solve the crossword puzzle.

Word List

red   brown   blue

green   orange

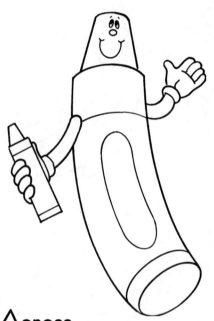

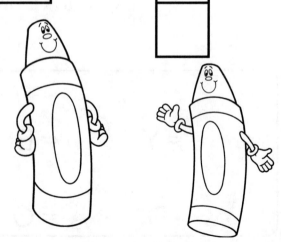

Across

3. A pumpkin is _____.
5. A fire truck is _____.

Down

1. The sky is _____.
2. Chocolate is _____.
4. Grass is _____.

38   © Carson-Dellosa Publ. CD-6875

Use the secret code to solve the riddle.

What do you get when elephants stampede through an apple orchard?

A p p l e s a u c e

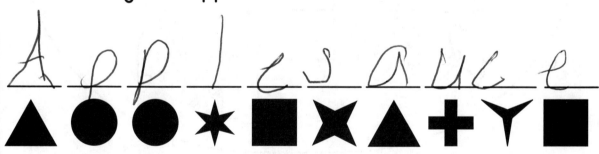

Secret Code

★ = L ✚ = U Y = C ✖ = S

● = P ▲ = A ■ = E

Use the word list to solve the crossword puzzle.

Word List

castle   pet   fish   gills   guppy

Across

2. A small fish is a ____.

4. The fish swam through the ____ in the fishbowl.

Down

1. A ____ lives underwater.

2. Fish breathe through ___.

3. A fish makes a nice ____.

Use the secret code to solve the riddle.

What do you call a sleeping bull?

B U L L D O Z E R

Secret Code

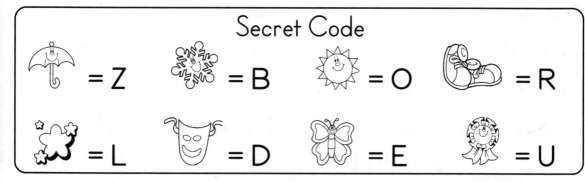

| ☂ = Z | ❄ = B | ☀ = O | 👟 = R |
| 🌸 = L | 😈 = D | 🦋 = E | 🏵 = U |

Use the word list to solve the crossword puzzle.

Word List

sail

swim

waves

boat

blue

Across

1. Water is ____.

2. The ____ at the beach were rough.

4. A ____ moves the boat.

Down

1. A ____ floats in the water and carries people.

3. I'd like to ____ like a fish.

Use the secret code to solve the riddle.

What kind of fish is rich?

A G O L D F I S h

Secret Code

☆ = S   △ = O   Y = H   ○ = F

⬠ = L   ✚ = I   人 = G   ⬡ = D

Use the word list to solve the crossword puzzle.

Word List

wake   alarm   ticks

time   watch

Across

1. My clock _____ loudly.
4. When the _____ goes off, it's time to get up.

Down

1. Seven o'clock is the _____ that I wake up.
2. In the morning, I _____ up and get ready for school.
3. I wear a _____ on my wrist.

Use the secret code to solve the riddle.

How do you keep a skunk from smelling?

    !

Secret Code

 = S   = H   = O   = N

 = L   = D   = E   = I

Use the word list to solve the crossword puzzle.

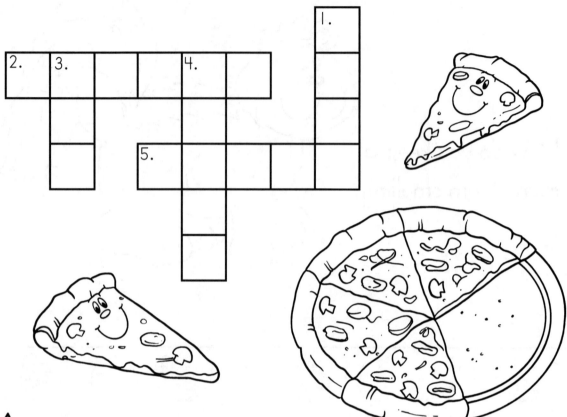

Across

2. I like ____ on my pizza.

5. A ____ has cheese and tomato sauce
   on top.

Down

1. I like to drink ____ with my pizza.

3. Pizza is best fresh and ____.

4. I can only eat one ____ of pizza.

Word List

soda

pizza

cheese

hot

slice

Use the secret code to solve the riddle.

What do whales have that no other sea animals have?

R A B Y _____ W H A L E S _____

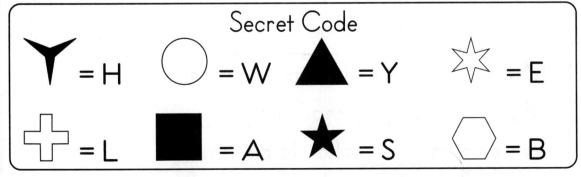

Secret Code

Y = H   ○ = W   ▲ = Y   ☆ = E

✚ = L   ■ = A   ★ = S   ⬡ = B

Use the word list to solve the crossword puzzle.

Word List

| post | bag | dogs |
| stamp | letter | |

Across

3. Lick the _____ and put it on your letter.
5. I will write a _____ to my aunt.

Down

1. Mail carriers should watch out for biting _____.
2. Mail carriers carry mail in a _____.
4. We go to a _____ office to buy stamps.

Use the secret code to solve the riddle.

What has one horn and gives milk?

A M I L K T R K

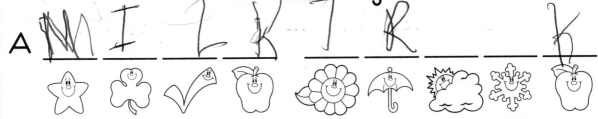

Use the word list to solve the crossword puzzle.

Across

1. You need to put _____ in a gumball machine.
3. I like to _____ gum.
5. I can blow a _____ with my gum.

Down

2. You can't chew gum at _____.
4. I like minty _____ best.
6. Can you _____ a bubble?

Word List
blow
chew
coins
bubble
gum
school

Use the secret code to solve the riddle.

What two things can you not have for breakfast?

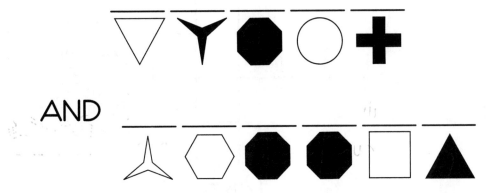

AND

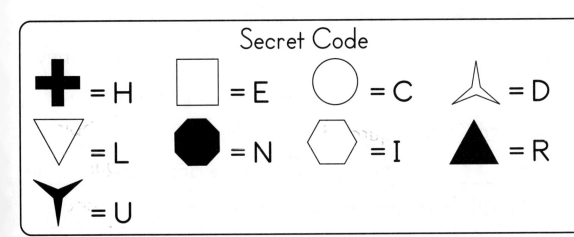

Secret Code

✚ = H □ = E ○ = C ⅄ = D

▽ = L ⬣ = N ⬡ = I ▲ = R

Y = U

Use the word list to solve the crossword puzzle.

Word List

lions   rings   top   bears   tent   circus

Across

2. A circus is held under a big ____.
4. Acrobats and animals perform in a ____.
6. The ____ are big cats with long manes.

Down

1. The ____ are big, furry animals that like honey.
3. A circus tent is also called the big ____.
5. There are three ____ in a circus.

Use the secret code to solve the riddle.

What do you get when you cross a bee with a bell?

A _hummdinger_

(handwritten below: hamdinger)

Secret Code

🌸 = H 🍀 = E 🍎 = N 👹 = U

🦋 = I ☀️ = G 👟 = D 💕 = M

🎀 = R

Use the word list to solve the crossword puzzle.

Word List

sun
pail
ball
shovel
sand
beach

Across

1. We play with a beach ____ in the pool.
3. Beaches have lots of ____.
4. I use a ____ to dig up sand and put it in my pail.

Down

1. We like to play in the sand at the ____.
2. We put sand and water in a ____.
4. You might get burned if you stay in the ____ too long.

54

Use the secret code to solve the riddle.

Which fork does a
farmer like best?

A _p_ _i_ _t_ _c_ _h_ _f_ _o_ _r_ _k_

Secret Code

✓ = H	☂ = T	✿ = K	☀ = I
♡ = F	★ = C	❄ = O	🍎 = R
☺ = P			

Use the word list to solve the crossword puzzle.

Across

1. Lettuce, tomato, and dressing make a ____.

3. We eat dinner on a ____.

4. I like potato ____ with my sandwich.

Down

2. These small insects love picnics.

4. Throw your paper in a trash ____.

5. We like to picnic in the ____.

Word List

park

chips

salad

ants

table

can

Use the secret code to solve the riddle.

How should a dentist
examine an alligator's teeth?

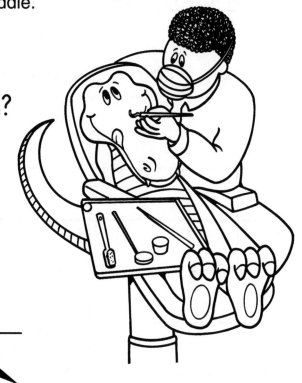

Secret Code

⅄ = Y	⬠ = E	☐ = C	★ = V
● = L	✦ = A	Y = F	■ = R
▲ = U			

Use the word list to solve the crossword puzzle.

Word List

brush   paint   draw   red   house   colors

Across

3. Red, blue, and green are all ____.

4. The color of strawberries is ____.

6. I like to ____ with watercolors.

Down

1. You can paint the walls inside your ____.

2. I use a ____ to put paint on the paper.

5. I like to ____ pictures with a pencil.

Use the secret code to solve the riddle.

What do you get
when you cross a frog
with a dinosaur?

A _ _ _ _ _ _ _

_ _ _ _ _ _ _

Secret Code

▽ = G   ⅄ = L   Y = E   ○ = I

□ = R   ☆ = P   ⬠ = D   △ = Z

⚝ = A   ⬡ = N

Use the word list to solve the crossword puzzle.

Word List

sun	seed
rain	dirt
plants	leaf

Across

1. If you plant a ____, a flower or vegetable will grow.

3. Flowers, trees, and vegetables are all ____.

6. Water that falls from the sky is ____.

Down

2. Seeds are placed in a hole and covered with ____.

4. The new ____ was bright green.

5. The bright, warm ____ helps all plants grow.